ELECTRICITY *and* POWER

MAKING SENSE *of* SCIENCE

Peter Riley

FRANKLIN WATTS
LONDON•SYDNEY

First published in 2005 by Franklin Watts
96 Leonard Street, London EC2A 4XD

Franklin Watts Australia
45-51 Huntley Street, Alexandria, NSW 2015

Text copyright © Peter Riley 2005
Design and concept © Franklin Watts 2005

Series Editor: Rachel Cooke
Editors: Kate Newport and Andrew Solway
Art director: Jonathan Hair
Designer: Mo Choy

Picture credits:
Adrian Cole: 17tr. Davies/Topham: 15t. Dimplex: 16t.
Mary Evans Picture Library: 25b. Firefly Productions/
Corbis: front cover inset. Simon Fraser/Science Photo
Library: 23b. Image Works/Topham: 27. Erich Lessing/AKG-Images: 5b.
Larry Mulvehill/Image Works/Topham: 11tr. Picturepoint/
Topham: 17bl, 18tr. Red Green Blue New Media Ltd,
Gonta/Alamy: 18bl. Harmut Schwarzbach/Still Pictures: 28b.
Science Museum, London/HIP/Topham: 4t, 13.
Wiliam James Warren/Corbis: 19t. Ron Watts/
Corbis: 28t. Kent Wood/Still Pictures: front cover main, 1, 9b.

Picture research: Diana Morris

All other photography by Ray Moller.

Every attempt has been made to clear copyright.
Should there be any inadvertent omission,
please apply to the publisher for rectification.

A CIP catalogue record for this book
is available from the British Library.

ISBN 0 7496 5531 3

Printed in Malaysia

CONTENTS

IT'S AN ELECTRIC WORLD

How many switches have you pressed today? The first switch might have been your bedroom light, then perhaps you turned on the radio. In the kitchen, you might have pressed down the toaster and flicked on the kettle. We use electricity all the time without thinking about it. But when there is a power cut, the television goes blank, the lights go out and you may have no hot water or central heating. Suddenly, you begin to realise how much we rely on electricity in our everyday lives.

Most of us know some basic facts about electricity – for example, that it flows through wires. We also know to be very careful with mains electricity, as it can be dangerous. But most of us would not know how to produce electricity, or how to make an electric light. This is not surprising because it took many years of scientific research for scientists to begin to understand electricity, and even longer before inventors found ways of producing electricity and making simple devices such as light bulbs (see page 17).

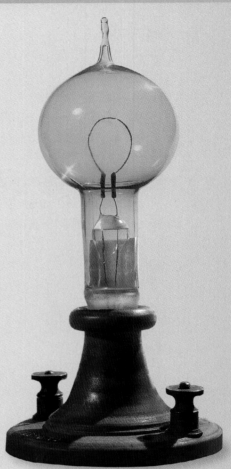

It is only in the past 150 years that scientists and inventors have learnt how to harness and use electrical power. Electrical devices, such as this early filament lamp, came into a few homes in the 1870s.

Most of us rely on electricity for light and entertainment at home.

ELECTRIC HOMES

Go through each room in your house and count up the number of things that need electricity to work. Do not forget that your water may be heated by electricity. Even if it is not, the pump that powers the central heating – and the timer that switches the water heater on and off – will be electric.

ELECTRICITY, ENERGY AND POWER

Electricity is one of our most important sources of energy. Energy is the ability to do work.

Power is the rate at which energy is used to do work. A powerful machine uses energy more quickly than a less powerful one. Electrical power is measured in volts. You may have come across the word 'volts' if you have bought batteries for a torch. The batteries have to be the right voltage (give the right amount of power) for the torch to work properly. If the batteries have too little power, the torch bulb will not light up. With too much power, the bulb will overheat and blow out.

Batteries come in a range of sizes. Generally, the larger the battery, the higher the voltage.

CURRENT AND STATIC

The electricity that we use to do work for us is current electricity – this electricity is produced by a battery or comes from the mains, and it travels through wires (see pages 10–11). However, the first sort of electricity to be discovered was static electricity.

'Static' means still, and static electricity stays where it is. This is the kind of electricity that can give you a mild electric shock when you touch a metal door handle after walking across a nylon carpet. Static electricity is also what makes it possible to stick a balloon to the wall after rubbing it hard on your jumper.

Amber is a hard, clear, yellowish material. It is actually the hardened sap of conifer trees that lived millions of years ago.

The Ancient Greek philosopher Thales (about 634–546 BC) was one of the first people to notice that when amber is rubbed, materials such as straw and feathers stick to it. He may have first noticed this when watching women spinning wool. Greek women often used amber spindles. These held the wool threads tightly when they were being spun into yarn, and this made the yarn easier to spin.

Today, we know that rubbing amber generates static electricity, which attracts the threads of wool. The Greek word for amber is electron, and it is from this word that we get the word electricity.

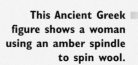

This Ancient Greek figure shows a woman using an amber spindle to spin wool.

5

STATIC ELECTRICITY

Tear some paper into tiny pieces. Put them on a table. Rub a plastic pen on your sleeve, then hold it close to the paper. The pieces of paper will jump up and stick to the pen.

This experiment is another demonstration of static electricity. Rubbing the pen on your sleeve gives the plastic of the pen an electric charge. When you hold the pen close to the paper, the paper is attracted to the pen and it jumps up and sticks to it. Seeing if an object will pick up small pieces of paper is one way of telling if it has an electrical charge. However, there are other ways of detecting static electricity.

A COMPASS FOR ELECTRICITY

One of the first instruments that could detect static electricity was called a versorium. It was made by the English scientist William Gilbert (1544–1603). The versorium was a type of 'compass' for electricity.

It was made from a metal pointer, mounted on a wooden stand, that could swivel in a circle like a compass needle. The pointer would swivel to point towards any object that had a charge of static electricity.

William Gilbert used his versorium to divide substances into electrics (substances that developed static electricity when rubbed) and non-electrics (substances that did not develop static electricity).

MAKE YOUR OWN VERSORIUM

Gilbert's versorium was made of wood and iron, but you can make one from two materials that were not discovered in his time – Plasticine and aluminium.

Place a lump of Plasticine on a board. Stick a plastic knitting needle into it, point up. Cut a strip of aluminium foil 4 centimetres by 12 centimetres and fold it down the middle. Balance it on the point of the needle. Rub objects made of different materials (for example a pen, a key, a balloon or a lemon) and bring them close to the aluminium. If they possess static electricity, the aluminium will move, just like the iron of Gilbert's versorium.

POSITIVE AND NEGATIVE

Through their experiments on static electricity, Gilbert and other scientists discovered that different charged materials behave in different ways. Some materials attract each other and stick together when charged. But other materials, or two charged pieces of the same material, seem to repel each other (push away from each other).

This behaviour of materials – some repelling each other and others attracting each other – happens because different materials develop different electrical charges when they are rubbed. Some materials get a positive charge, while others get a negative charge. Two materials with the same charge repel each other, but materials with opposite charges attract each other.

INDUCING A CHARGE

The idea of positive and negative electrical charge explains why materials that are charged attract or repel each other. However, it does not explain why, in the experiment at the start of this spread, uncharged pieces of paper are attracted to the charged plastic of a pen.

When a charged object is brought close to an uncharged material, the charged object makes an opposite charge in the uncharged material. This is called inducing a charge.

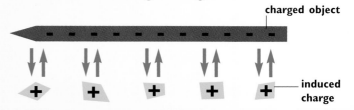

charged object

induced charge

THE **PHOTOCOPIER**

The American scientist Chester Carlson (1900–1968) invented a process called xerography, which is used in most photocopiers. A drum inside the photocopier is charged with static electricity. When light from white areas of the document being copied shines onto the drum, it destroys the charge. The printing on the document does not give out light so it forms a pattern of charge on the drum. When a powder, called toner, in the machine is sprayed onto the drum, it sticks to the electrically charged areas and makes a copy of the printing on the drum. This is transferred onto sheets of paper which pass through the photocopier.

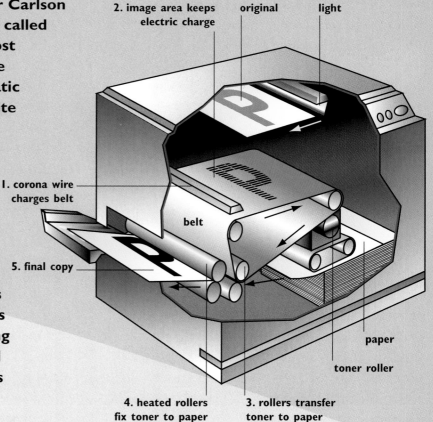

2. image area keeps electric charge

original

light

1. corona wire charges belt

belt

5. final copy

paper

toner roller

4. heated rollers fix toner to paper

3. rollers transfer toner to paper

We have already seen how rubbing some materials can charge them with static electricity. But what is electricity, and how does rubbing something charge it up? To find the answer, we have to look at the tiny particles that make up all materials.

All materials are made from very small particles called atoms. Each atom has a nucleus at its centre, surrounded by incredibly small electrons.

Some of the particles in the atom are electrically charged. In the nucleus, there are positively charged particles called protons. The surrounding electrons are negatively charged, and are attracted to the protons in the nucleus.

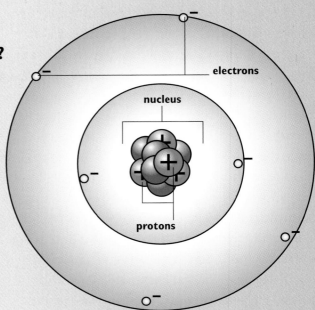

A diagram showing the structure of an atom. In a real atom, the nucleus and the electrons are much further apart.

RUBBING OFF ELECTRONS

When a material is rubbed and an electrical charge builds up, electrons are rubbed either onto or off the material. When polythene is rubbed with wool, for instance, electrons rub off the wool and onto the polythene. This makes the polythene negatively charged. When perspex is rubbed in a similar way, it loses electrons to the wool and becomes positively charged.

ELECTRONS ON THE MOVE

Eventually, a charged object will lose its charge because electrons always try to move from an area of negative charge to an area of positive charge.

You may have noticed that sometimes a jumper crackles when you put it on or take it off. The rubbing of the cloth against your body causes static electricity to develop on the jumper. In some places, so much charge develops that it cannot stay still. It passes through the air, making a crackling sound. In the dark, you can see tiny sparks as the electrical charge moves.

ELECTRICAL STORMS

In a storm cloud, air currents swirl upwards and rub ice crystals together. They become charged with static electricity, and the base of the cloud becomes negatively charged. Eventually, the charge on the cloud becomes so great that a huge spark passes through the air – a flash of lightning. The enormous 'crackle' caused by the spark is thunder.

ELECTRIC CURRENT

When electrons move from one place to another, it produces an electric current. A lightning flash is an enormous current passing through the air.

More often, electric currents pass through wires. For an electric current to flow, the wires have to be connected in a circle, or circuit.

American scientist Benjamin Franklin (1706–1790) proved that lightning is electricity. He famously flew a kite in a thunderstorm and used it to collect electricity from a storm cloud. This was dangerous and could have killed him.

Other scientists in Franklin's time thought there were two kinds of electricity (positive and negative), but Franklin suggested that there was only one. He thought that when a material was charged with electricity, it either received too much electrical fluid and became positively charged, or electrical fluid drained from it, and it became negatively charged.

CAN YOU MAKE A CIRCUIT?

Take a battery, three wires, a bulb and a switch. Connect the battery, the bulb and the switch together in a circle, using the wires. You should have made an electric circuit. Close the switch: does the bulb light up?

ELECTRONS AND CURRENTS

The English scientist William Crookes (1832–1919) experimented with passing electricity through vacuum tubes. He found that strange rays could be made to travel across the tubes. Another English scientist, Joseph John Thomson (1856–1940), performed a range of experiments on the rays. Thomson concluded that the rays were made from tiny particles. He called the particles electrons. This led to the idea that a current of electricity was a current of electrons.

Have you ever looked closely at a wire used for carrying electricity? The outside of the wire is plastic, while the centre is made of metal. The electric current travels through the metal, while the plastic cover stops electricity from passing through.

Metals, and other materials that allow electricity to flow through them, are called conductors. Materials such as wood and plastic, which do not allow electricity to pass through them, are called insulators.

WHAT MAKES A GOOD CONDUCTOR?

Metals are good conductors because some of the electrons in a metal are not held tightly to the nucleus, and can move easily through the metal. When an electric current flows, the electrons move along a wire at a speed of a few millimetres per second.

Insulators do not have freely moving electrons. All the electrons in their atoms are held firmly in place around the nucleus. This means that it is difficult for electrons to move through the material.

TESTING CONDUCTORS AND INSULATORS

Set up a circuit with a battery, a bulb and four wires. Leave a gap in the circuit. Try using different materials in the gap to complete the circuit. Arrange the materials into two groups – those that make the bulb work (conductors), and those that do not (insulators).

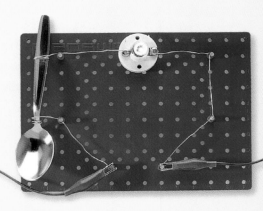

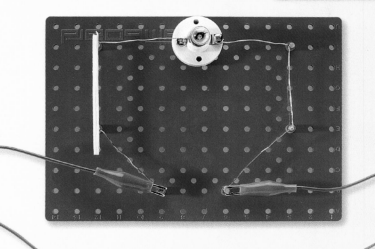

RESISTANCE

Although electrons can flow through a conductor, they do not flow completely freely. As electrons move through the conductor, they collide with atoms and also jostle together like people leaving a football game. The property of a conductor that opposes the flow of the current is called resistance. A long wire has more resistance than a short one, because there are more atoms to get in the way of the flowing electrons. A thin wire has a greater resistance than a thick wire, because there is less space for electrons to flow and they move more slowly – like motorway traffic having to use a single lane because of roadworks.

VARY THE RESISTANCE

The 'lead' inside a pencil is actually made of graphite. Although it is not a metal, graphite is a conductor. Soak a pencil in water to make the wood softer, then remove half the pencil to expose the graphite. Make a circuit with a 4.5 volt battery, a bulb and wires. Connect one end of the graphite to the bulb with a wire. Touch the wire from the battery to the other end of the graphite. Then, move this wire along the graphite and watch the bulb change in brightness.

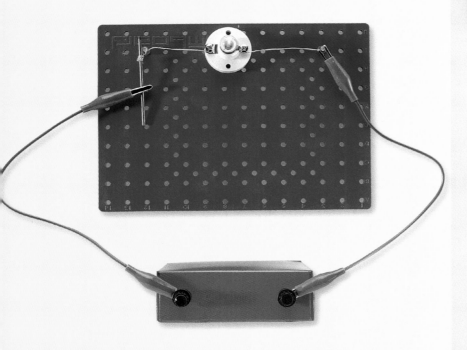

WORKING OUT A LAW

Georg Ohm (1787–1854), a German scientist, investigated the flow of current through wires of different lengths and thicknesses. He found that the size of the current depended on the voltage of the battery and the size of the resistance in the wire. The way voltage, current and resistance are related is known as Ohm's law, and the unit of resistance is called the ohm.

SUPERCONDUCTORS

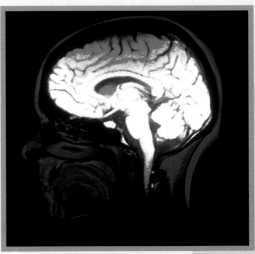

The most important part of an MRI scanner is a strong magnet. Using superconductors, engineers can make these magnets smaller and more powerful.

Superconductors are materials that have no resistance to a current flowing through them. This means that they can carry more powerful currents than ordinary conductors.

Superconductors are important parts of MRI scanners – machines used in hospitals to give detailed pictures of the inside of the body. Superconductors are also being developed for use in maglev trains (see page 27).

MEASURING CURRENT

When a current is moving in a circuit, its size can be measured. The size of a current is the rate at which electrons flow through the conductor. The unit of measurement of electric current is the ampere (A). A current in which six million million million electrons flow past a point on the conductor every second, is a one ampere current.

CELLS AND BATTERIES

How many of your belongings need a battery to make them work? Perhaps there is one on your wrist right now – your watch. A battery is a portable source of electricity. But how does it produce electrical energy?

A single battery is more correctly called an electrical cell, and a battery is actually a group of electrical cells joined together.

HOW CELLS WORK

There are three main parts to an electrical cell. They are the negative electrode, the positive electrode, and a chemical or mix of chemicals separating them – the electrolyte. The electrodes are usually two different metals.

When a cell is connected into a circuit, chemical reactions take place inside it. The negative electrode reacts with the electrolyte to produce electrons, which flow out through the negative terminal. At the same time, electrons come into the cell at the positive terminal. A reaction between the positive electrode and the electrolyte uses up these electrons.

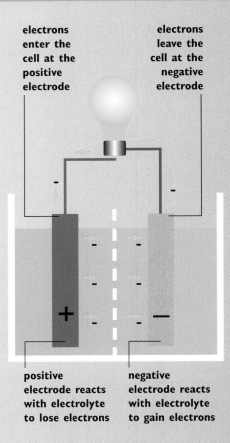

electrons enter the cell at the positive electrode

electrons leave the cell at the negative electrode

positive electrode reacts with electrolyte to lose electrons

negative electrode reacts with electrolyte to gain electrons

THE DRY CELL

The most common type of electrical cell is the dry cell. In a dry cell, the positive electrode is made of graphite, the material used in pencils. The outside case of the battery is the negative electrode: it is made of the metal zinc. The electrolyte is a thick paste between the two electrodes.

LEMON POWER

Push a large steel nail and a brass screw into a lemon. Attach a wire to each one and connect them to a 1.5 volt bulb. The lemon works as a battery: the juice is the electrolyte and the metals are the electrodes.

RECHARGEABLE BATTERIES

Cells only produce electricity for a certain amount of time. Then the chemicals powering the cell run out. Some kinds of cell are rechargeable – they can be charged up from the mains so that they work again. The nickel/cadmium cell is a rechargeable kind of dry cell. The battery in a car is a rechargeable battery: it is made up of a number of electrical cells. The electrodes are made of lead and lead dioxide, and the electrolyte is an acid, sulphuric acid.

You should never try to recharge batteries that are not labelled rechargeable.

BATTERY POWER

As we saw on page 5, the power of a cell to push electrons round a circuit is measured in volts, after the scientist Alessandro Volta (see panel). Many cells have a voltage of 1.5 volts. However, most electrical devices need more power than this to work. The solution is to use more than one cell, connected together to give a larger voltage.

Luigi Galvani (1737–1798), an Italian scientist, studied the muscles in frogs' legs. When he applied a spark to a pair of legs, they twitched. He also found that the legs twitched when he connected them to two metals, such as iron and copper. From this, he concluded that muscles contain electricity. Alessandro Volta (1745–1827), another Italian scientist, believed that electricity could be generated without the muscles. He found that if he dipped a piece of copper and a piece of zinc in salt water, he got a current. This was the first electrical cell. Later, Volta made the first battery, using cells made out of a disc of copper separated from a disc of zinc by a disc of cardboard soaked in salty water. Volta piled many of these cells on top of each other to make a powerful battery called a voltaic pile.

Alessandro Volta. The battery, or voltaic pile, he invented is on the left on the table in front of him. The object on the right is Volta's invention for measuring static electricity, similar to a versorium (see page 6).

CIRCUITS

You are surrounded by electric circuits. They run in the walls around you to the plug sockets and light switches, and across the ceiling to the lights themselves. In the kitchen, there are circuits in the fridge, microwave, kettle and toaster. There are also circuits in your alarm clock, computer and television. Each circuit is designed to perform a particular task.

The things that make up an electric circuit are called components. The components in a light circuit are lights and switches. In a kettle, the switch and the heating element are the main components. In a radio or CD player, there are many components, including loudspeakers to play back the sounds. But in all circuits, one rule always applies. The components have to be wired together so that electricity can flow from the battery or mains, through the components and back to the battery or mains again.

SERIES AND PARALLEL

There are two ways in which components can be arranged in a circuit – either in series or in parallel. In a series circuit, all of the components are connected one after the other in a line. In a parallel circuit, the components are arranged side by side.

When two or more components are arranged in series, the resistance of one component is added to the resistance of the next. This makes it more difficult for the current to flow, and the size of the current falls.

When components are arranged in parallel, the resistances of the different components do not add together, and the size of the current does not fall. However, a parallel circuit with several components uses more power than a series one, so the battery will run out more quickly.

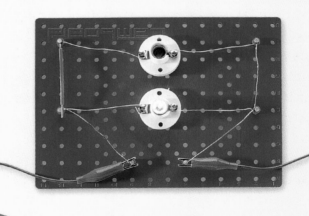

In this series circuit, the current follows in one path, passing through each component in turn. With one bulb missing, the circuit is broken so the other bulb is not illuminated.

In this parallel circuit, the current flows along two different paths. One bulb can still be illuminated even though the other is missing.

The large number of components in a device like this radio are held together on a circuit board. The components are connected to each other by thin strips of metal. Some are in series and some are in parallel.

WHEN A BULB BLOWS

Christmas lights are an example of another way in which series and parallel circuits differ. Some sets of Christmas tree lights are wired up so that all the bulbs are in series. If one of the bulbs blows, the lights will not work at all until the faulty bulb is replaced. However, most Christmas lights are wired in parallel. If one bulb blows, it does not break the circuits of the other bulbs. Your Christmas lights keep on shining – and it is much easier to find and replace the broken bulb!

Parallel circuits are widely used because of this advantage over series circuits. They are used in street lights and circuits in the home. Imagine what would happen if series circuits were used. A damaged street light could black out a town, and a blown fuse in an iron would shut down the television, the lights and the fridge.

MAKE YOUR OWN CIRCUITS

Predict what will happen when you set up a circuit with one bulb in it then add a second in series. Predict what will happen when you set up a circuit with one bulb in it then add a second bulb in parallel. Do your observations match your predictions?

CIRCUIT DIAGRAMS

It takes a long time to draw a picture of a circuit, and sometimes, the connections are not clear to see. Electrical engineers get round this problem by using circuit diagrams. These diagrams show the connections clearly, and are quick and easy to draw once you know the symbols for the different components.

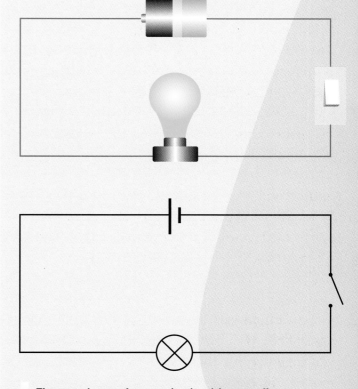

The top picture shows a circuit with one cell, one bulb, one switch and three connecting wires. Below it is a circuit diagram of the same circuit.

For an electron, moving through a wire is like tackling an obstacle course. The electrons have to get round the atoms in the wire, and often they knock into the atoms and make them vibrate. If the atoms vibrate strongly, they give out heat and light.

In many electric circuits, the heat and light produced by the flow of electricity is a nuisance. Electrical devices sometimes need fans to cool down the circuits, to keep them working properly. But some devices, such as light bulbs, electric kettles, cookers and heaters, are built to produce heat or light.

A long, thin, straight wire gives out a lot of heat, but it is spread over a large area. In an electric heater, the wire is tightly coiled to make the heat more concentrated and useful.

When a light bulb is lit, it glows so brightly that it is almost impossible to see the filament at all (upper picture). However, if you look closely at a clear bulb when it is switched off, you can see that the filament is a coiled wire (lower picture).

DIFFERENT METALS

The copper metal used to make most wires is no good for making heaters, because when it gets hot, copper reacts with oxygen in the air and burns out. So, the heating elements in kettles, cookers and electric fires are made from nichrome. This is an alloy of nickel and chromium that can glow at red heat in air without damage.

An electric light bulb has a thin wire called a filament inside. When a current passes through the filament, it becomes so hot that it produces a bright white light.

The filament in a light bulb needs to be able to withstand temperatures far higher than the element in an electric heater. The filament is made from a metal called tungsten. Tungsten can be heated until it is white hot without melting. However, if tungsten is kept at a high temperature in air, it soon burns out. To prevent this happening, the filament is enclosed in a glass bulb filled with a gas called argon. This gas does not react with the hot tungsten, so the metal does not burn out.

LOOKING FOR LIGHT

We depend on electric lamps to light our homes at night, but do you know exactly how many you have? Make a guess, then go round your home and count them. How close was your guess to the actual number of lamps?

BLOWING A FUSE

All electrical appliances are designed to work with a certain size of current. If the current is too high, the appliance may be damaged. It could overheat and start a fire. As a result, in some countries, plugs have fuses. Fuses also protect the electrical system in cars. A fuse is a thin metal wire. It is designed to melt when the current passing through it becomes too high. When the fuse wire melts, it breaks the circuit and current stops flowing. Checks can then be made to find out why the fuse blew.

The fuse panel in a car.

Thomas Edison in his laboratory with some of the electric filament lamps he invented. He and Swan later worked together to develop light bulbs.

INVENTORS OF THE FILAMENT LAMP

In 1860, Joseph Swan (1828–1914), an English scientist, tried to make an electric light using a filament of carbon. This burnt up quickly in air, so Swan tried to create a vacuum in a glass bulb around the filament. However, he could not remove all the air from the bulb and the filament only glowed for a short time. During the 1870s other scientists discovered how to make better vacuums. In the late 1870s, both Swan and an American inventor, Thomas Edison (1847–1931), were able to make light bulbs that worked.

ELECTRONICS

We live in an electronic age. Computers, televisions, CD players, games consoles and mobile phones are all electronic devices. Electronics is a way of using tiny electric currents to do useful jobs.

A wire, a switch and a bulb are electrical devices. They do not control how the current flows through a circuit; they simply let the current pass through. On the other hand, electronic components control the flow of current in a circuit in some way.

ELECTRIC COMPONENTS

One electronic component is a diode. A diode lets current move through it in only one direction. Diodes are used to protect electronic circuits. In a radio or CD player, for instance, there is a diode circuit that stops electricity going into the device if you accidentally connect the wires the wrong way round.

A light-emitting diode (LED) is a special kind of diode that lights up when current flows through it. LEDs have many uses, from forming the numbers on a digital clock to making the picture on a giant television screen.

SHRINKING THE COMPONENTS

Shockley (seated), Bardeen (left) and Brattain (right) at work on the apparatus that they used to develop the first transistor.

Sir John Ambrose Fleming (1849–1945), an English electrical engineer, discovered that electricity would pass in only one direction through vacuum tubes (see page 9). From his discovery, the first diodes were made: they were called valves. The American Lee de Forest (1873–1961) invented another kind of valve that worked as an amplifier.

William Shockley (1910–1989), an English–American physicist, worked with the American scientists John Bardeen (1908–1991) and Walter Brattain (1902–1987) to produce tiny amplifier valves made from the material germanium. These components became known as transistors.

TRANSISTORS

Transistors are probably the most important electronic components. They are used in two main ways. A transistor can control the flow of an electric current by switching it on and off. It works as a tiny, very fast switch. Transistors can also be used to convert a small current flowing through one circuit, into a large current flowing through another – they amplify the current. The amplifiers in sound systems and many other devices rely on transistors.

CONTROLLING CURRENT FLOW WITH SWITCHES

There are many circuits in electronic devices, and the flow of electricity through them is controlled by switches. Two circuit arrangements of switches are the AND circuit and the OR circuit. In an electronic circuit the switches are transistors, but you can make a similar circuit using a battery, two switches and a light bulb.

Make an AND circuit by wiring the two switches and the bulb in series, following the circuit diagram (below left). What do you have to do to light the bulb? Now make an OR circuit with the two switches in parallel (below right). Can you see why it is called an OR circuit?

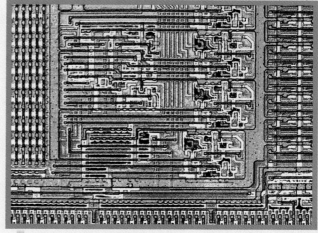
The miniature components on a silicon chip.

In electronic equipment such as mobile phones, computers and televisions, many different components are crammed together on a tiny piece of silicon the size of your little fingernail. The silicon and its circuits are known as a microchip.

Silicon is used for microchips because, by making chemical changes to small areas of the silicon, it is possible to make different electronic components. The components are connected together by covering the whole chip in a thin layer of aluminium then etching (scraping) away most of the layer to leave just the electrical connections.

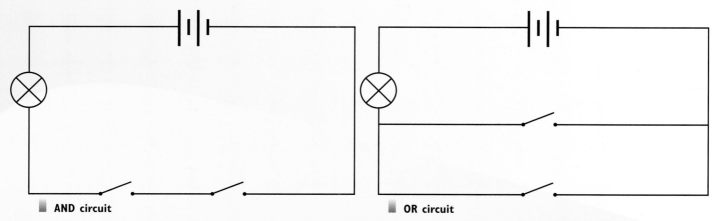

AND circuit

OR circuit

MAGNETS AND ELECTRICITY

Do you have a magnet on your fridge? What is it doing? Some people have them holding letters and postcards, or you may use a magnetic alphabet to write messages.

Like all magnets, fridge magnets cling to iron and steel (fridge doors are made of steel). The magnetic force can act even with a non-magnetic material (such as a postcard) between the magnet and the iron or steel.

MAGNETIC POLES

Fridge magnets are often small discs or thin strips. A bar magnet (below, left) is better for studying magnetic properties in detail. Near each end of a bar magnet is a place where the magnetic force is very strong. This place is called a pole.

If you hang a bar magnet so that it can swing, it acts like a compass. One end faces north, while the other end faces south. It does this because the centre of the Earth itself behaves as if it were a huge magnet, attracting your smaller one. The end of a bar magnet that faces north is called the north (north-seeking) pole; the other end is

the south (south-seeking) pole. Opposite poles of two magnets attract each other, while poles that are the same repel.

LOOKING AT MAGNETIC FIELD

The region around a magnet, where its force pulls on magnetic objects, is called its magnetic field.

Put some iron filings in a plastic bag and seal it. Place the bag on a white card and spread out the iron filings inside the bag. Then, put the card and bag over a bar magnet and see the magnetic field pattern produced by the iron filings.

EARLY EXPERIMENTS ON MAGNETS

Peter Peregrinus, a French scholar who lived in the 13th century, named the poles of a magnet north and south. He noticed that like poles repel and unlike poles attract each other. He found that when iron filings were placed near a magnet they spread out in a special way. Today we call this the magnetic field pattern. William Gilbert (see page 6) showed that a magnet could dip down as well as point north, and suggested that the Earth was like a huge spherical magnet.

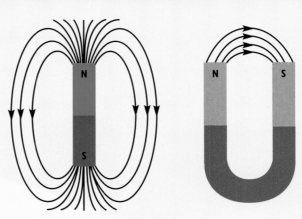

The magnetic field pattern of a bar magnet and a horseshoe magnet.

MAGNETISED AND UNMAGNETISED

Magnetic materials, such as iron and steel, contain millions of groups of atoms called domains. These all behave as if they were tiny magnets. In an unmagnetised piece of metal, the domains face in all directions, like the people at a pop concert when the stage is empty. When a metal becomes a magnet, all the domains line up and face in the same direction, just like people watching their favourite band.

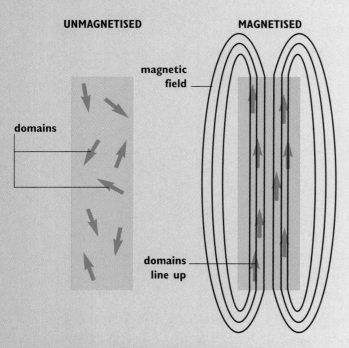

UNMAGNETISED   MAGNETISED

domains

magnetic field

domains line up

CONNECTING ELECTRICITY AND MAGNETISM

Fridge magnets and bar magnets seem to have little to do with electricity. But magnetism and electricity are closely connected. When an electric current passes through a wire, it makes a magnetic field around the wire.

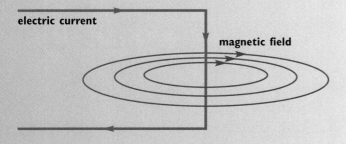

electric current

magnetic field

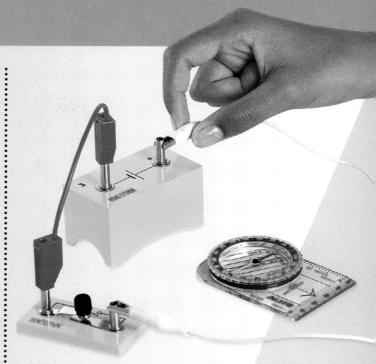

A CURRENT AND A COMPASS

Set up a circuit with a switch, a 4.5 V battery and a wire. Put a compass close to the circuit while it is switched off. Now turn on the circuit and watch the compass needle.

What happens if you reverse the current (turn the battery around)?

MAKING THE CONNECTION

Hans Christian Oersted (1777–1851), a Danish scientist, used a current of electricity from a voltaic pile (see page 13) to investigate electricity and heat. In one experiment, he accidentally brought a wire close to a compass, and the compass needle moved. Oersted was the first to recognise the connection between electricity and magnetism.

ELECTROMAGNETS

We saw on the previous page that when a current of electricity flows through a wire, it makes a magnetic field. When magnets are combined with electricity, they have many important uses.

When a current of electricity flows through a wire, it makes a circular magnetic field around the wire. If the wire is made into a coil (a solenoid), when electricity flows through it, the coil behaves like a bar magnet. It has a north and south pole and a magnetic field around it. This kind of magnet is called an electromagnet.

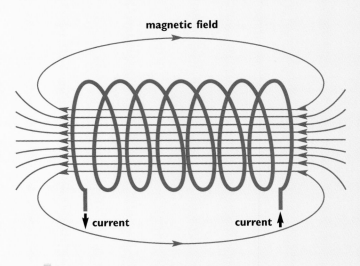

magnetic field

current   current

■ The magnetic field through a solenoid.

KEEPING AND LOSING MAGNETISM

A piece of steel can be made into a magnet by putting it into a strong magnetic field. When the steel is taken out of the magnetic field, it stays magnetised: it is a permanent magnet. But a piece of iron does not behave in the same way. When iron is in a magnetic field, it becomes a magnet. But once it is out of the magnetic field, the iron loses its magnetism. This property of iron is extremely useful when making electromagnets.

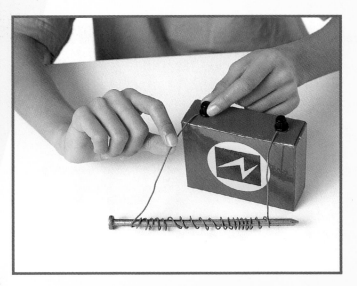

EASY TO CONTROL

As we have seen, a solenoid is a simple electromagnet. But the magnetism it produces is quite weak. If you put a piece of iron in the middle of the solenoid, things change. When a current passes through the solenoid, it magnetises the piece of iron, too. The solenoid and iron together make a much stronger electromagnet. When the current is switched off, the iron is no longer in a magnetic field, so it loses its magnetism. This means that an electromagnet can be controlled by simply switching the current through the solenoid on and off. This allows electromagnets to be used for many purposes.

COILS AND STRENGTH

Wind a few coils of wire around a large iron nail and connect the wire into a circuit with a 4.5 V battery. Bring the nail near to some steel paper clips. How many paper clips does the electromagnet pick up? Add some more coils of wire to the nail and repeat. Does the electromagnet increase in strength?

FROM EYES TO CHIMES

Electromagnets are used in hospitals. If a person gets a piece of iron or steel in their eye, it can be removed using an electromagnet.

Powerful electromagnets attached to cranes are used for lifting and moving cars in a scrap-yard. To pick up a car, the crane operator rests the electromagnet on the car, then switches it on. It can then be lifted and placed on a stack. To release the car, the crane driver simply switches off the electromagnet.

When your doorbell or school bell rings, there could be an electromagnet at work. In many electric bells, an electromagnet is being switched on and off to make a hammer hit a bell or door chime.

Andre Ampère (1775–1836), a French scientist, showed that the magnetic force produced by a wire depended on its size and the direction of the current in it. He also suggested that a solenoid could behave as a magnet. The English scientist William Sturgeon (1783–1850) tested this idea, and added a bar of iron to the centre of the solenoid. This was the first electromagnet.

■ A powerful electromagnet in a scrap-yard crane.

It takes about 4.5 volts of power to light up two or three bulbs in a school experiment. So, imagine how much power is needed to light all the lights in a city.

Add to this all the televisions, cookers and other electrical devices, and you soon realise that supplying electricity to a city needs much more power that we can obtain from cells or batteries. We get this power from electricity generators at a power station.

ELECTRICITY FROM MAGNETS

On pages 22–23 we saw that a current of electricity can be used to make a magnet. The reverse is also true – a magnet can be used to generate a current of electricity. There is a magnetic field around a magnet, and if this is made to change close to a wire, a current of electricity is generated in the wire. The magnetic field can be made to change by moving the magnet past the wire. Only a very small amount of electricity is generated this way, but if the magnet is made to move inside a coil of wire, a much larger current can be made.

WATCH THE NEEDLE!

Place a compass in the tray of a large matchbox, and wrap a long piece of wire around the tray 20 times (make sure you can still see the compass). Coil another long piece of wire to make a solenoid with about fifty turns in it that is big enough to fit a large bar magnet inside. Connect the ends of the wires together but keep the two coils well apart. Push a bar magnet slowly into the solenoid and watch the compass needle as you do so. Pull the magnet out and watch the needle again. If a current of electricity is made, the needle will move.

A BETTER GENERATOR

The amount of electricity made by a generator can be increased if the magnet is moved quickly. The way to do this is to spin the magnet within the solenoid. A power station generator contains a large electromagnet that spins at 3,000 times per minute inside huge coils of wire. An electromagnet is used instead of a magnet because its magnetism is easier to control.

GENERATOR FUEL

A generator needs some sort of power source to turn the magnet or the coil. Most power stations use coal or oil as a source of energy. The heat from these fuels heats water and makes steam. This pushes its way over turbine blades attached to the generator, which then make the electromagnet spin.

Using coal or oil can harm the environment, and there are only limited amounts of these fuels: one day they will run out. Scientists and engineers are looking at alternative sources of energy to use in power stations, such as wind and water power.

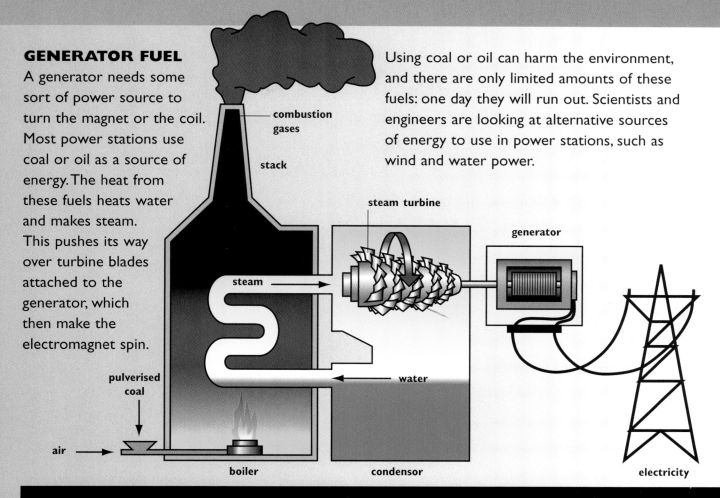

combustion gases

stack

steam turbine

generator

steam

water

pulverised coal

air

boiler

condensor

electricity

THE **FIRST ELECTRICAL GENERATOR**

An engraving of Michael Faraday. The apparatus on the left was one he developed to generate electricity.

Michael Faraday (1791–1867), an English scientist, studied the work of Ampère and Sturgeon (see page 23) and wondered if magnetism could generate electricity. He wrapped a coil of wire around one part of an iron ring and connected it into a circuit with a battery. He wrapped another coil of wire to a different part of the ring, and connected it to a current-measuring device called a galvanometer. When he switched the current on and off in the first coil, the galvanometer showed that a current was produced in the second coil. The ring's changing magnetic field as the current was switched on and off generated electricity in the second coil.

ELECTRIC MOTORS

When was the last time you used an electric motor? Was it spinning a CD in your stereo or turning gently a meal in a microwave oven? Electric motors, like electricity itself, are so widely used we hardly notice them. Inside an electric motor, magnetism and electricity work together to provide a spinning motion that has many uses.

HOW A MOTOR WORKS

The inside of a motor is almost the reverse of the inside of a generator. A coil of wire spins in the middle of the motor, and it is flanked by two magnets. The north pole of one magnet and the south pole of the second magnet face the coil. The coil is attached to an electric circuit.

When a current flows through the coil, it becomes an electromagnet, with a north pole at one end and a south pole at the other. These are attracted to the north and south poles of the magnets surrounding the coil. If this was all that happened, the coil would move a short distance and then stop. But a device, called a commutator, on the end of the coil, switches the current round in the coil as it spins. The current in the coil is reversed, which reverses the positions of the north and south poles. Now they are repelled by the poles of the magnet, and the coil spins on.

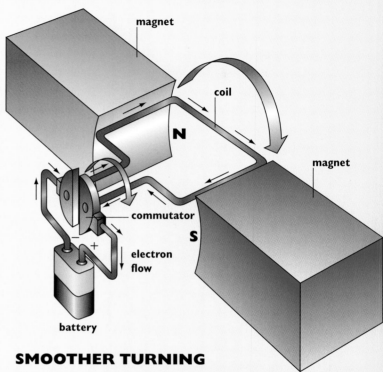

SMOOTHER TURNING

Most electric motors are a little more complicated than the one described here. They have several coils on the shaft so that each one is pushed and pulled at different times from the others. This makes the shaft spin more smoothly.

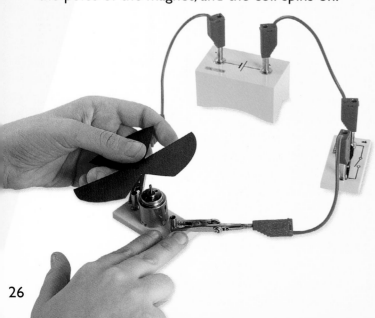

KEEP COOL

Set up a circuit with a battery, a switch and a motor. Cut out a circle of card and draw lines to divide it into six. Then, cut along the divisions almost to the centre of the card to form the blades of a fan. Twist each blade a little to make the fan. Make a hole in the centre of the fan and attach it the shaft of the motor with sticky tape. Now test your fan. Does it cool you down? If you have the graphite pencil from the challenge on page 11, use it to change the resistance in the circuit. How does this affect the motor and fan?

The first electric motor was invented by Michael Faraday (see page 25). It had a magnet standing on end in a bowl of mercury. A wire hung down from above the magnet and dipped into the mercury. The wire and the mercury were connected in a circuit to a battery. When a current passed though the wire, it moved round the magnet.

Faraday's motor could not be used to drive machines. Joseph Henry (1797–1878), an American scientist, invented the electric motor we use today.

A FLOATING MOTOR

Many electric motors are similar in basic design, but different in size and power. The motor in a model electric train is similar to the one in a real electric locomotive.

One kind of electric motor that is very different is called an induction motor. It is used in a few trains running on special tracks known as maglev trains. Maglev is short for magnetic levitation. Powerful electromagnets in the train repel the special track beneath the train so strongly that the train rises off the ground and appears to levitate (float in the air). The electromagnets on the train and magnetic regions on the track also produce other forces that move the train along.

■ A maglev train floating along its track.

We depend on electricity for so much of our power that it would be difficult to live without it. Even when you go camping, the chances are you will have a torch that runs on batteries. We live in the age of electricity.

ELECTRICITY BEFORE BREAKFAST

Before you have breakfast, you could have experienced electricity that is generated in three different ways.

You may have generated electricity this morning when you got dressed. The rubbing as you put on your clothes can sometimes produce static electricity, which crackles and makes tiny sparks.

If you have an electric toothbrush, it will use electricity generated by chemicals. The electricity comes from batteries in the toothbrush handle.

If you have a shower, or turn on a light or the radio, you will use mains electricity that is generated in a power station using magnets.

Electric torchlight shines in a tent at night.

MOVING POWER AROUND

Electricity produced in power stations has to be moved around the country to the places where it is needed. The electricity travels through overhead power cables, supported high in the air by metal pylons. Between the cables and the pylons, there are stacks of ceramic (pottery) discs. The discs are very good insulators that prevent electricity from flowing into the pylons themselves.

Not all power stations use coal or oil to turn the generators. This power station uses nuclear power.

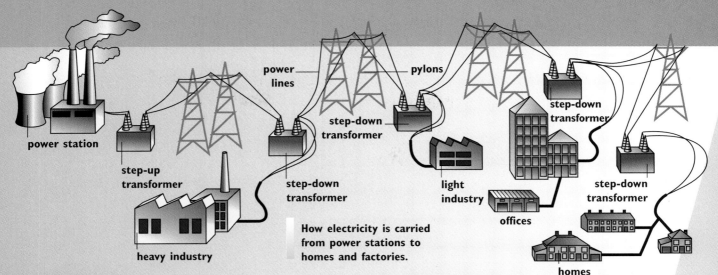

power lines

pylons

step-down
transformer

power station

step-up
transformer

step-down
transformer

light
industry

offices

step-down
transformer

step-down
transformer

heavy industry

homes

How electricity is carried
from power stations to
homes and factories.

CHANGING THE VOLTAGE

A power station generator produces electricity with a voltage of 25,000 volts. As electricity is moved from the power station to where it is needed, the voltage is changed many times, using devices called transformers.

When the electricity first leaves the power station, transformers raise the voltage to a massive 400,000 volts. The reason for this is that when the voltage goes up, the amount of current flowing goes down. With a high voltage, the cables carrying the electricity can be thinner because they are carrying less current. A smaller current also means that the wires heat up less.

FROM PYLONS TO YOUR HOME

When the electricity reaches a town, it passes through other transformers that reduce the voltage. For factories such as steel works that need a lot of power to run their machinery, the voltage is reduced to 33,000 volts. For industries that need less power, such as factories making shoes, the voltage is reduced further to 11,000 volts.

Some offices and small workshops use electricity at 415 volts, while for shops and houses, the voltage is reduced to 240 volts.

SAVING POWER

Many countries have a large number of power stations. At the moment, great amounts of coal and oil are used to generate electricity, but these power supplies are running out, and new ways of generating electricity are being investigated. The supplies of fuels can be made to last longer if people do not waste electricity.

THE FIRST TRANSFORMER

As well as making the first generator and the first motor, Michael Faraday (see pages 24–25), also invented the first transformer. He found that electricity passing through a coil of wire on an iron ring could produce an electrical current in a second coil of wire around the same ring. Nikola Tesla (1856–1943), a Croatian-American electrical engineer, used Faraday's discoveries to invent the transformers we use today.

CAN YOU SAVE POWER?

Look at times when you waste electricity by leaving things on that are not in use. How often do you leave on a light or leave the television on standby? Work out how many hours of electricity you could save by switching off.

TIMELINE

Thales (about 634–546 BC), a Greek philosopher, was one of the first to describe static electricity.

Peter Peregrinus (13th century), a French scholar, named the poles of the magnet and studied magnetic fields with iron filings.

William Gilbert (1544–1603), an English scientist, invented the versorium 'compass' for detecting electric charge.

Benjamin Franklin (1706–1790), an American scientist, proved that lightning is electricity by flying a kite in a thunderstorm.

Luigi Galvani (1737–1798), an Italian scientist, suggested that muscles contain electricity.

Alessandro Volta (1745–1827), an Italian scientist, made the first electrical battery. The volt is named after him.

Andre Ampère (1775–1836), a French scientist, showed that the magnetism produced by a wire depended on its size and the direction of the current in it. The amp is named after him.

Hans Christian Oersted (1777–1851), a Danish scientist, discovered that electricity and magnetism are connected to each other.

William Sturgeon (1783–1850), an English scientist, made the first electromagnet.

Georg Ohm (1787–1854), a German scientist, worked out how voltage, current and resistance are related. The ohm is named after him.

Michael Faraday (1791–1867), an English scientist, made the first electrical generator, the first transformer and the first electrical motor.

Joseph Henry (1797–1878), an American scientist, invented the electric motor that we use today.

Joseph Swan (1828–1914), an English scientist, tried to make an electric light using a carbon filament. He later worked with American inventor **Thomas Edison (1847–1931)** to invent the modern light bulb.

William Crookes (1832–1919), an English scientist, found that strange rays travelled across vacuum tubes when electricity was passed into them.

Sir John Ambrose Fleming (1849 –1945), an English electrical engineer, worked out how to control current flow using vacuum tubes.

Joseph John Thomson (1856–1940), an English scientist, discovered electrons.

Nikola Tesla (1856–1943), a Croatian-American electrical engineer, used Faraday's discoveries (see above) to invent the transformers we use today.

Lee de Forest (1873–1961), an American inventor, made a vacuum tube into an amplifier.

Chester Carlson (1900–1968), an American scientist, invented xerography, a process in which static electricity is used to make photocopies.

Walter Brattain (1902–1987) and **John Bardeen (1908–1991)**, both American scientists, worked with **William Shockley (1910–1989)**, an English-American, on the invention of transistors.

GLOSSARY

acid – a sour, sharp or corrosive substance. Lemon juice and vinegar are mild acids.

alloy – a mixture of two or more metals.

atoms – the very tiny particles that everything is made of.

battery – a combination of two or more electrical cells.

charged – a material is said to be charged if it has more electrons than normal or fewer electrons than normal.

chemical reaction – the process in which substances join together or split apart to produce new substances.

component – part of an electric or electronic circuit that controls how the current flows through it.

conductor – a material that allows electric charge to pass through it.

current – the flow of electricity through a circuit.

diode – a component in an electronic circuit that lets the current pass in only one direction.

dissolving – when a solid mixes with a liquid and breaks up into small pieces that cannot be seen.

electrical cell – a device that produces electricity from chemicals (see also battery).

electrode – a conductor in an electrical cell.

electrolyte – the chemicals in an electrical cell between the positive and negative electrodes.

electron – a tiny, negatively charged particle in an atom.

filament – a very thin thread.

germanium – a material that is used to make microchips and other electronic components.

heating element – a wire designed to give out heat when electricity passes through it.

induced charge – an electrical charge generated in a material when another charged substance is brought close to it (but not touching).

insulator – a material that does not allow electric charge to pass through it.

magnetic field – the region around a magnet where its magnetic force pulls on magnetic materials.

nucleus – the centre of an atom.

power – the rate at which something can do work.

proton – a positively charged particle in the nucleus of an atom.

repel – push away.

resistance – the ability of a material or an object to slow down the free flow of electrons in an electric current.

solenoid – a coil of wire.

static electricity – an electrical charge that stays in one place.

transistor – an electronic component that can act as a switch or as an amplifier.

turbine – a fan with many blades, that are pushed round by steam, water or air.

voltage – the power of a cell, battery or generator to deliver electricity.

INDEX